A
BEAUTIFUL
MESS

pyrokardia

A BEAUTIFUL MESS

DEDICATION

This book is dedicated to all my followers on Instagram
for the love and making me believe in myself

A BEAUTIFUL MESS

A BEAUTIFUL MESS

CONTENTS

ACKNOWLEDGMENTS

I'll like to acknowledge the efforts of my friends for taking the time to read through the drafts notwithstanding their busy schedules. I really appreciate you guys and thanks for the brainstorming for book titles, even though I didn't end up using anyone, please don't kill me (hahaha).

PYROKARDIA

AUTHOR'S NOTE

Poetry is such a personal art and everyone interprets a poem differently. Titling a poem can force an interpretation in a specific path, so I'm leaving all the poems untitled with a blank space and you can fill in a title that speaks to you personally. If you would like to know my choice of title, you can go to the back and check out my own choice of title for each poem. I do hope you enjoy reading them as much I loved writing this pieces of me in words.

A BEAUTIFUL MESS

Loving you is full of confusion
Sometimes I think I hate you
More than anything in the world
Sometimes I'm totally in love with you
And I would destroy the world for you
Makes me sad and then happy
My mood fluctuates like the waves
But if I'm the stormy sea
Yours is the cliff I always want to crash into

I want to breathe
Life into you
Straight from my thoughts
My heart will be the power
Behind your creation
And you'll be mine
A sum of my needs
And all I ever wanted
The bad, the good and the ugly
A living embodiment
Of the inadequacies of my thoughts
And the purity of my heart
Alas, when the wind blows
You'll be gone with it

If I could live a thousand lives
I'll spend every single one loving you
But I still don't think
I can ever love you enough
As much as you deserve to be loved
Even if I could combine
A thousand lifetimes of loving
Into a single lifetime of love

I used to spend my nights
drinking from your lips
Getting drunk on love
Memorizing every part of you
And every morning
always seem more beautiful
than the last.

Now the lips of these bottles
fill my nights
Getting drunk on the pain
Trying to replace the memories
of the taste of your lips
And every morning
seems so much sadder
than the last

A BEAUTIFUL MESS

I've been broken
Too many times
I've lost count
It's my default now

My wall is in disrepair
Cracks running across its face
Geckos and lizards slipping in and out
Carrying infestations of sadness

Trying to fix myself
With one night stands
And random steamy flings
Ended up widening up my cracks instead

I stand alone
Patrolling my walls
Fixing up the cracks and broken hinges
With self-love

Safe behind these walls
My cracks fixed, gates sealed up
Alone, but I'm happy
And that's all I ever needed

I stay up most nights

Thinking of you
While trying not to think about you

Missing you
While trying not to miss you

An Angel filled with grace and poise
She strutted into my life with grace
Paused at the entrance with a dignified pose
Her presence making my heart race

An Angel, that's what she is to me
With hair flowing down her shoulders
The stirrings she evokes in me
Making my body shake with the shivers

An Angel created to inspire me
To loftier heights than I ever hoped to reach
With her right beside me
Every obstacle becomes an easy pitch

An Angel to grant me peace
To calm my troubled waters
Even without speech
In her presence my worries waiver

An Angel to make me complete
As life's pendulum swings
To add or to delete
With her it's all winnings

An Angel for me to cherish
To treasure all my life
With you, I'm already rich
Beyond blessed with you in my life

Today I admit to myself
That I do miss you
Not what we had
But the fantasy
Of what I imagined
We could have had
Causing me throbs
From six feet within my heart
Where it now lies

My heart is infested with maggots
Wriggling around inside it
Making my heart ugly and rotten
Slipping out into my stomach
Causing me pains
Giving me heartache
Then you came
Bringing sunshine into my heart
And they went into molting
Curling up in cocoons of change
Emerging into something beautiful
Giving me butterflies in my stomach

I was but a mirror
A magic mirror on your wall
There to boost your ego
An outlet for your temper
Broken into pieces
Over and over again
But still, I gave you everything
Reflecting to you
Only the best I had in me
My cries to you were silence
Never to be heard
I wonder if you even see me
If your reflection isn't all you see
I'm just a tool to you
I only exist when you need me
Only there to be used
To serve your will

Let me love you
As the sun loves the moon
Shinning so intensely
Every single time we meet
That the entire world
Is set aflame
From the brilliancy
Of our touch

A BEAUTIFUL MESS

It's a beautiful new dawn
I wake up confused
Cause my bed feels empty
And I wonder why
Is it cause my heart feels hollow?

There's a fist shaped hole in it
From when you reached into me
With your smiles and your shy kisses

Now I feel incomplete without them
I miss you babe
Come complete me once again

I knew you
Even before I met you
You visited my dreams
In several lands and realms

You were mine
Made from the divine
Even before time
To be my prime

Knew from where you hail
Down to your DNA
Knew about your smiles
Knew about your trials

Yet my eyes perceive you not
Though you're forever in my thought
Filling up my mind
To your presence I'm blind

The love of my lifetimes
I know not for what crimes
We could never be together
Forever to ache for the other

Destined to be apart
Forever seeking the path
To bridge the distance
And bring us to coexistence

In each other arms
To share memoirs
In front of the hearth
Never to be apart

I stand in front of the mirror
Trying to see my reflection
But all I see is you
The pieces of me I changed for you
Trying to make you stay
But you never did

I'm sick
Fallen down to an illness
The greatest ailment
That has ever plagued humanity

It is a disease of the mind
When it's acute, it's called lust
It can be cured
By your kisses and your body

When it's chronic, it's called love
It's beyond any cure
It can only be managed
By regular doses of your mind and soul

So darling
Will you be my nurse?

A BEAUTIFUL MESS

I find comfort in this song
And from the lyrics
Stream forth a flow of memories
Sending echoes into my mind
Dredging up the embedded thoughts
Until all I hear are the strains
Of our love's dirge

Glancing into your eyes
I'll see my reflected soul
Kissing your lips
I'll forget my fouls

My heart is set alight
Whenever you're close to me
I'll hold on tight
Forever to your hands

Whenever I see you around
My heart loses control
When I'm with you
My soul is made whole

When I'm without you
I'm like a sword without hilt
Without your touch
My soul wilts

My soul cries out
Where is my draught?
Without which
My flame dies out

I hate lies
Sincerely I do
But when you tell me
That you love me
I still smile

I imagined you perfect
I imagined you flawed

I imagined a vision
Amidst the darkness

I imagined you

A BEAUTIFUL MESS

They asked if I'm fine
I wanted to tell them my arms still seek your shape
beside me each night
That my body still seeks your warmth when the night
gets cold
That I wake up with my arms groping for you
That I still make breakfast for two
That I spend my days waiting for your call
And I sit quietly waiting by the door
Waiting for that creaking noise that you always hated
as the door opens
Hoping that you come back home
That I tend your garden
Wanting you to look down on our home from heaven
and see the flowers in bloom
I want to tell them that I replay the last conversation
we ever had
Wondering if you had a clue that when you banged
close the door as you left in anger
That you knew you were never coming back
And I stay up most nights wondering what I could have
said differently to have made you stay
Then maybe you wouldn't be gone from me
But they don't want to know all that
All they want, is to hear the words "I'm fine"

I loved till I l lost myself
And became just a part of her
Lost all sense of self
Till all that mattered was her

Just a tiny piece of the puzzle
The whole picture being her wants
Like the animals in a zoo
I was there only to satisfy her wants

So darling, please forgive me
If I seem reluctant to let go
Of what makes me, me
For the emotions I refuse to show

Have a little patience with us
For what I feel may be buried deep
But I promise this is no hoax
For if I'm ever without you, I'll weep

I've loved slow
I've loved fast
And there's no love
As painful as the slow

Sure the fast love is super intense
But it fades real fast too
Loving slow, is loving thoroughly
Loving with every piece of your soul

And when it burns
It burns away every piece of you
Leaving you nothing
But an empty hollow shell

Let's take this dance
Pull me close to you
And place your hands in my hands

Let's glide across the dance floor
As if we're moving amidst the clouds
Our moves will be without flaw

Let's dance under the stars
With a thousand twinkling lights shining on us
The rays illuminating our hearts

Let's kiss under the rain
Our hearts thumping to the beat of the rain drops
And it will wash away our pain

Let's spend the night under the moon
And wake up to grass stains and swollen lips
As we begin our first day as one

A BEAUTIFUL MESS

I miss you so much
You were my phoenix
Waking my heart
From the cold dark abyss
Into a wondrous world
With fiery wings
To keep me aloft
From the sharp serrated
Teeth of loneliness
And despair
You brought me back
To life
From the cold hands
Of death
You were the earth's green
Feeding my soul
With wondrous fruits
Keeping me from starving
From this parched soul
Of mine

I have a dream
Of a clear blue sky
Of a bright sunny day
Shining down on us

I have a dream
Of a beautiful melody
Of an eternity of time
As you walk down the aisle to me

I have a dream
Of glorious sunsets
Of beautiful sunrises
With you next to me

I have a dream
Of passionate kisses
Of soul warming embraces
As we make beautiful love

I have a dream
Of a radiant sunrise
Of fading shadows
Playing across your sleepy face

I have a dream
Of a garden
Of roses and tulips
Filled with our children

I have many dreams
Of the future
Of hallmark moments
Filled with you and I

I have so many dreams
Of tiny little dreams
Of everything my heart desires
And they are all about you

We built our relationship with our words
Laying them down
Brick by brick
Until the bridge is completed
After a while
We kept our words
Of everything that hurts to ourselves
Building a wall with the silence
Until we were but two cities
With a road in disrepair
And a massive wall of silence between us

I want you
Every single broken piece of you
I'll make an effigy from them
Set them on fire with my love
We'll dance by the flames
As we get drunk on our new found love

I'm the villain in my own story

Knocking off the bridge before it's completed
Sniping off the thread before it entangles me
Blowing off the flame before it engulfs me

Afraid of the unknown
Afraid to need you
Afraid to love you

I always thought
we had something magical
that we fitted together perfectly

But we were just an illusion
hiding our flaws behind lies
that bonded us together
only for a fleeting moment

Let the word walk off the board of your tongue
Dive in babe
Even if your words don't swim right
I don't need the eloquence
Set them free
And let me see what lies behind the curtains of your
mind
No dramas, no act
No staged plays
I want to know the truth
Set me free with your words
No matter how much they hurt me
They may break my wings
But I'll heal
I'll learn to fly again
Maybe without you
I'll find another's wings
To carry me home

My mind is split in two
Should I love you?
And risk the pain
Maybe, it'll be something beautiful

Or should I let you go?
And I'll be at peace
Without drama or pain
Wondering if we could have had something special

These are my choices
But are they mine alone to make
Do your wants or needs matter
Or do I make it all about me?

I survived your love
Your love didn't break me
It is the hope you gave me
That destroyed me

A BEAUTIFUL MESS

I keep on writing
Digging into my soul
Trying to get in deep enough
To find the right words

I keep on waiting
Bidding my time
Trying to find that fortuitous moment
To reach out to you

I keep on hoping
Trusting my instincts
Trying to find that event
That will make you notice me

I keep on dreaming
Feeding off my emotions
Trying to fulfill my deepest desire
To make you mine

I still stay up all night
The memories keep me up
Leaking out through my eyes
Unseen by anyone but me
Unfelt by anyone but me
Hiding with them in the dark corner
Where I'm cuddled up
Afraid of what the dreams will bring

The sound of my heart beat
The sway of her hair
The warmth of her body heat
The fragrance of the air

Every little thing about her
Makes her special to me
Changes the way things are
From what I used to be

A sedate state of calm
To a mix of jumbled feelings
Raging wind amidst the palm
Leaves swirling and twisting

She's everything I wished for
All I dreamed of
What more can I wish for?
She's the one I love

So many choked back words
Words that show my affection
How much I think about you
And how much I cherish you

So many choked back words
Words that would open me up
To your blank stares
And piercing silence

So many words I refused to speak out
Clenched behind my lips
Dying out without a pip
Never to be heard by you

So many words left unsaid
In the gap between my mind and my lips
Lying there just waiting
For the courage to open my lips

So many words I should have said
Of how much I loved you
Of how much you mean to me
But they were never heard by you

A BEAUTIFUL MESS

I sit on the porch
Under the moonlight
Without any torch
To provide any light

I recall the moments
We shared together
All the events
That we ever held dear

I treasured you
With loving words
Warm embraces
And passionate kisses

Our love wasn't perfect
But it was all I had
It was special
And all I ever needed

Your lies poison the air
Your hurtful words choking me up
In your mind
You think you're winning
When all you're really doing
Is reteaching my heart
How to survive on oxygen
Instead of you

Let's take a walk
Down the path of life
At the distance, we won't balk
Neither would we shrink from strife

Let's hold hands
As we walk through the storm
As the clouds darken and the leaves dance
We'll cuddle by the roadside and be warm

Let us skip together
Through fields of daisies
As we celebrate our years together
Maybe we'll meet some fairies

Let's take a run
Up and then down the hill
The world's whispers we'll shun
Though they chase and dog our heels

Let's take a step
Over the threshold of our home
And our roots will run deep
From our porch we'll watch the gloam

Do you remember our first kiss?
And how we promised each other
That what we had will last forever
No matter the adverse weather

I don't remember our last kiss
It was nothing special I guess
Just another thing I don't miss
We never had another like our first

Being with you is a dream
Of fantasies and mysteries
An adventure through time and space

You make me feel special
Without any apparent effort
Uplifting my soul into the clouds

I feel invincible with you in my life
A gladiator to conquer all
No matter the obstacles against us

It makes me so happy
Having you coursing through my veins
You're an addiction I never want to beat

Do I wonder about you?
About how life could have been
If you had stayed with me

Yes, I do
I spend so much time wondering
I have no time left to build another life

When I think of you
Everything just seems clear
For that single instant
I know everything that matters
See the world with perfect clarity
Understand the meaning of all things
And I can see the connections between all things
For that single moment
I know my place in the world
I guess my mind isn't equipped to deal with the
sensory overload
Cause every time I think of you
My mind goes blank

I poured everything I've got into you
And I got nothing back
Until I was empty and drained
Of all feelings for you
Cause you didn't refill me
Cause you gave nothing back
Now, there's nothing left to give
So I'll take my leave

One day our love will fade
But it's not this day

So, let's celebrate one more day
Of our love growing stronger
Our passion blazing brighter

When we won't hesitate to take on the entire world
If only for the tiniest possibility of being together

When any fight we have
Is only but foreplay to mind blowing sex

When we are all that matters
And our numerous flaws don't matter

One day this love will fade
Maybe it's tomorrow or the next

But for today
We'll scream our love
And the world will quake

We'll shout into the void
And our voice will echo for eternity
For we don't know what the future holds

So today we'll hold on to each other
We'll fight for each other
And we'll love
Like it's our last day

I knocked on your castle gates
Screamed, cajoled and begged
Hoping to make your heart my home
But your gates stayed closed

Tried climbing over your walls
But you pushed me off the top
Tried digging beneath your walls
And you collapse my tunnels

For six months I've waged war
Trying to ram your gates open
Looking for a crack in your wall
Through which I can slip in through

While you sit on your wall
Watching me with derision
Treating me like a fool
For wanting to make your heart my home

So now, I'm leaving
Leaving behind the gates of your stone-walled heart
Though I look back once or twice
Hoping you ride out to me

I know there are jeweled cities out there
And I'll find one with an open gate
That will welcome me with much joy and merriment
And there, will I make my home

I've written so many words
Sometimes I think too many
Trying to capture the way you make me feel
But I just can't find the right words
The perfect words to capture
The moments and the emotions
The feeling of completeness
And the tiny little things I can't explain
I've tried and I've failed
But I'll keep on trying
Room littered with crumpled pieces of discarded paper
Really, it's a mess
A reflection of the insides of my head
There are just no words for the chaos
And the beautiful strange order
You bring to my life
So I'm just going to write you
Every day for the rest of my life
Of the numerous little things you make me feel
And maybe when I'm long gone
You can make some sense
From a compilation of it all

Within a twinkle of an eye
So does time fly by
Emotions kept on high
The unshed tears
You couldn't keep in
As you hear yourself cry
From the sorrows and the pain
Each day, as the sun rises
Dispersing the shadows of darkness
You try to conquer the new fears
As the days roll on by
You sink lower into despair
Into a world filled with grey
A new life devoid of all colors
A life without you

Let me walk you home
I'll be the perfect gentleman
Making you laugh
Till the journey ends

Let me kiss you by your door
It'll be gentle, beautiful and deep
Submerging you in the depths of my passions
Till you come up gasping for air

Let me into your heart
I'll be the most amazing drug
Pumping through your veins
Till I'm diffused throughout your body

Let me into your life
I'll be your guardian angel
Your companion along life's path
Till our life's journey ends

I want to hold you in my arms
And never let go
You are my earth
And I'll be your moon
But you revolve around him
Cause he's your sun
Leaving me out in the cold
Devoid of all warmth
But still, I wait for you
And I'll be there
Through your darkest moments
I'll shine upon your darkness
And alleviate as much as I can
The darkness in your heart

A kiss shared with her
Is a collage of colors
Over life's blank canvas
Creating within silence
A cacophony of sounds
In which we find our rhythm

I stay in the silence
Listening to my heart beat
To its rhythm and it's beat
As it pounds and it thumps
Trying to figure out
If it still beats for you or not

She's beautiful
And she knows it too
Drawing my gaze with a powerful pull
Turning away will be a battle

She's the center of the room
The walls seeming to revolve around her
She's a goddess, I assume
Cause everything but her, becomes a blur

Like a moth to a flame
My feet drag me to her
Cause I really have to know her name
Though in my soul, I already knew her

In her light
I bask in her glow
My heart suddenly seems light
An effect of her hello

She's got the voice of an angel
To my ears, every single syllable was perfection
Unlike that of any other girl
To be her king will forever be my mission

At noon
when the sun is highest in the sky
and the world is awash in light
I tell the world I'm over you.

At midnight
when the moon is highest in the sky
and the world is cloaked in darkness
my heart tells me all about you

I want to experience a love
as vast and immense as space
with no visible start nor end
A love full of wonders and mysteries
Surrounded by angelic bodies
with the stars as our neighbors
A plethora of colors
bringing more vibrancy to our lives
we'll live like gods
Visiting times not of ours
through sinkholes

Goodnights sound a
lot like goodbyes
When it's with you

And the nights seem
to last forever
When it's without you

Hidden within the fogs of my dreams
Sat an ethereal beauty
Just beyond my arms
But still within reach

Gown as light and pale as the clouds
Silvery strands of the moonlight
Bathing on her golden skin
Sets my thoughts alight

Infused with my desire
A figment of my thoughts she may be
She still set my vision's edges afire
A dream match it will be

I wonder how it will be
If I could have a real girl so fine
But only in my dreams she'll be
And there she would always be mine

Do I really need love?
Do I need the games?
The pains, the fights, the dramas

I keep telling myself no
That I don't
That I can survive without it

I only need myself
But by the end of the day
I find myself back in your arms

I'm nothing but a fool
Unable to take my own advice
And you're nothing but fool's gold

We argue
We believe
We fight
We love

That's who we are
Sticking to each other
Through the ups and the downs
Fighting and loving one another

Loving through the pain
So we can cherish the joys
And even with tears running down my face
My lips would still whisper "I love you"

I keep thinking
I keep trying
To bring out beauty from what we almost had

The only beauty were my dreams
Of you and I

The reality of you and I
Was filled with ugliness

I'm an addict
Not to drugs
They give me no joy
And their euphoria is finite

I'm addicted to you
The euphoria of you
Running through my veins
Overwhelming my heart

Till all it beats for
Is the next dose from your lips

Every day
I go out of my way
Hoping not to come across you
Avoiding every place
that I can meet you at
Avoiding every place
that reminds me of you

Every night
Before I go to bed
You're all I think about
And I hope I get to see you in my dreams
Cause in my dreams
You're still mine

There's this feeling you give me
I can't call it love
Love is for fools
What you give me
Is beyond that
It's the most beautiful feeling
That I've ever felt
You bring me peace
To my mind, body and soul
A point of order within my life's chaos
And that's something I don't ever want to lose

Each night
I curl up in a corner
Embraced by the darkness

Fight off sleep as long as I can
Cause within these dreams
The nightmares lurks

Waiting for me to close my eyes
To torment me
With memories of your face

The smiles I've lost
And the buttery legs kisses
You always give me

As I toss and turn
Trying to correct my mistakes
To make you mine again

But I'm caught within these loops
Of recreating every single step I took wrong
My dreams are all nightmares now

Be mine
Don't be like the moon
Hanging all alone in the dark night sky

Be mine
Shine just for me
And I'll adorn you with the stars

I remember the first time
Our first kiss
How it felt so perfect
Even though it was shy at first

Our passions wiped our hesitations away
Slowly but surely wrapping us in a cocoon of perfection
We couldn't seem to have enough
We had everything we needed in that moment

Now everything else matters but us
All our kisses are chaste and hurried
Leaving a bitter aftertaste in our mouths
A memory of what was once perfect

Sometimes she's the storm
Sometimes she's the calm
But always she's the wind
Filling up my sails
Propelling my heart
Toward her distant shores

If I had known
That would be our last kiss

Maybe I would have kissed you
Just a few seconds longer

Maybe I would have held you
Just a few seconds longer

Maybe it would have made you stay
Maybe it would have saved your life

She's got the eyes
The kind that scares me
That promises forever
Without saying a word
A forever of falling
With no guarantee of ever being caught

They say loving is a risk
Is it a risk worth taking?
The heartbreaks and the pain
The games and the betrayals
And what if your love is unrequited
Can you deal with the loneliness?
Of seeing your loved one with another
I wonder if you're strong enough
To keep breathing if your heart breaks
Or are you going to melt into a puddle of your tears
Love is a risk
With stakes too high for me
Take your love and find another player
I'll rather live my life in peace
Without love's chaos

They say loving is a risk
But just living is a risk
Every day is a risk
I could literally just die
At any moment
Even by just lying on my bed
They say loving is a risk
But what is life without risk
A life without meaning
A life without joy
So I'll love and I'll live
With every breathe I take
Until the risk takes me
And I'll die gladly
Knowing I lived fully

I'm tired
I'm tired to the bone
You make me wish my bones break
Just to escape the pain
Trying to seek succor
Under another type of pain
Hoping that it will provide a relieve
But it doesn't
It never does

I really want to write about you
How you make me feel
How beautiful you are to me
But the words never seem to come
Not cause I've got nothing to say
Or because I don't know what to say
I guess, I'm just scared
That if I put it to paper
It will suddenly be too real
And my heart will be at risk again
So forget about my silence
The empty crumpled paper sheets
Listen to my heart beats
And know that they beat only for you

My heart was broken once
And from that I have learnt
Though it may weigh ten ounce
To be safe I have it kept

In a glass jar
So the world may know
My heart is not ajar
It is mine alone to own

No longer may it be broken
It is entrusted to no one
Nor can it be woken
It is not to be found

Never again will it get bruises
Safe from love's heat
And passionate embraces
My jarred heart

They told me to beware
that you've got a heart
as black as night

So I became the moon
lighting your path
to our home in the woods

PYROKARDIA

You told me
I wasn't man enough for you
That what you want
Is someone more in control of his emotions

That showing you love is weakness
And you left me for another
A man in control of his emotions
A stone hearted man

Gave him everything
And you got nothing back
Forgetting the fact that
A stone provides no sustenance

Instead, he cracked open your heart
And ate it all
Like a nut and its shell

Now you're back
Shedding tears of regrets
Wanting this mushy fruit heart

But I'll wash my heart in your tears
And devour it entirely in front of you
Cause I've got none to share with you anymore

Leave me a trail
of the broken pieces
of your heart

And I'll find my way
home to you

Gathering every piece
to make you whole again

Our love rose with the dawn
The rays slicing between our defensive curtains
Waking our emotions from the bed

Our love shined like the midday sun
The heat warming up our lives
Burning up our insecurities and fears

Our love waning with the setting sun
Fading into the horizon
Sinking into the depth of the ocean

Our love disappeared into the night sky
Wispy tendrils of cold seeping into my heart
Freezing the tears running down my cheeks

I love you deeply
Totally and wholly
Even though I don't know why

Trying to reason it out
Because you don't believe it's real
Yet, it just simply is true

Love you even if you don't
And there's nothing I can do about it
It has a life of its own

I've got no control over it
Maybe one day, I'll learn to
And then I'll be able to let go

Standing in a room full of people
Yet, I've never felt so alone
With earpiece in my ears
Listening to my sad songs
Merging with the sorrowful melodies

My heart is burning
I never can understand
Why it's called heart break
Cause it seems whole to me

I know, because it hurts so much.
I can feel every inch of it
And they're all in flames
From the fire you created in me

Now you've left me
And the fire is out of control
Consuming my soul

So, here I am
Trying to drown out these flames
With these bottles

I started life
As a shadow
Gradually gaining substance
Trickles of reality
Molding me into shape
But devoid of color
Until I met you
And you colored me in
With the passionate hues of your love

I kept hoping
I kept holding on
Thinking you're going to change
Maybe you just needed time
Making excuses for you
Not wanting to break my own heart
The lies slowing suffocating me
Till I can't breathe near you
And I called it love
But it's not
It's nothing but lies
Nothing but the stink
Of your lies
Choking me up
Stinging my eyes
As I force back the tears
And slowly it dawned on me
I'm going to asphyxiate to my death
If I keep staying here with you
Constantly doused in the musk of your lies

Dark hair on a golden body
Her lips stained by my life's blood
Her bosom shaped to caress my head
The feel of her hair
Like silk to my touch
Her eyes bottomless pools of sunshine
Her fragrance so alluring
With you, I feel alive
Like I'm pumped full of hypnotics
My love, your cherubic image
Stimulates my sensory neurons

I still want to tell her
That I love her
That my every single thought is filled with her
presence
That I still dream of her lips
That when I look towards her and see her smiling
It still makes me happy
I want to tell her
That my heart has grown over the knife she stuck into
it
Making it a part of it
My heart bleeds every time it beats
My heart beats for her
My heart bleeds for her

Our love is a dream
Of stolen kisses
Of whispered secrets
And midnight walks

Loving in the darkness
Hiding our emotions
In the light of the day
The sun knows not that we're lovers

Like the werewolf
Our love is unleashed
By the moonlight
Howling our love to the moon

Love is an invading army
Sending enemies spies to sneak past my walls
To turn my own heart against me
Convince it to open up my gates to it forces
Then come marching in
Amidst much glory and fanfare
Trumpets blaring and colorful parades
Fooling me to relax my guard
Then it does what all armies do best
Cast me down from my throne
Raid my stores for its sustenance
And burning down my structures
When it's all done
And marching on to the next city
All you see of me
Is the smoke rising from my destruction

There she is...
A dream turned reality
A goddess turned mortal
An angel to shelter my heart
To complete the jigsaw puzzle
That is me

PYROKARDIA

Every time I look at you
I'm flooded with memories

Of us under the rain
Of passionate kisses shared

How you would smile at me
Like I was all that mattered

How you clung to me
Afraid to go over the edge

Our body molding together perfectly
As we found warmth in each other

Each time I look at you
My heart breaks all over again

For what we have lost
For what I have lost

Stay here with me
In this moment
Of our own making
A moment of serenity
Of two souls entwined
In peace and harmony
Out of time stream

Every sunrise seems to remind
Me, of all I've lost
Every subtle shift of the wind
On my skin, feels like your touch

Precious memories of you
And every moment I've lost
All we went through
Cherished and yet the worst

Cause I don't want to remember
What you meant to me
Just an ember
Of your thought set me aflame

I'm tired of the vicious cycle
The fights and the silence
Wrecking my psyche
Breaking through my defense

There are so many stars
In the night sky
Each beautiful and unique
Shining bright on us
But none could ever
Shine into my soul
Light up my heart
Like the stars in your eyes

I wish you had asked me
Instead of assuming I didn't care
I wish you had told me you loved me
Instead of being afraid to say it

I want you to tell me
Whisper it into the winds
And let the waves bring them to me
To my heart's alcove

A refuge for you and I
Away from the ravages of time
Where you'll always be young and beautiful
Where you'll always be mine

Loving you is a choice
I made within me
To endure the pain
The games and the lies
That I never wanted

With brief flashes of intense joy
That wipes out my memories of previous hurts
Fading them into oblivion
With every taste of your lips
With every touch of your skin
Making me feel special

And in those moments
Nothing else matters but you

PYROKARDIA

I wonder what you want from me
Served you my heart on a silver platter

And I watched you devour it
Eating daintily with your forks and your knives

Watched you stab me down
Watched you cut me off

And during every single second of it
I gazed at you with love

As you ate your fill of me
And tossed the rest in the trash

Don't love me back
the way I love you
that's not what I want
I want to give you my all
and I want you to give me
all you've got too
Even if it's not much
as long as you give your all
I've got everything I need

I will fight the world
for our love

I will not fight you
to love me

After all the time we've spent together
You'll think I'll be jaded by now

Seen all your faces
Heard all your stories

But, every day with you
Still feels like a mystery

I'm still enchanted by your face
I'm still laughing at your stories
I'm still falling in love with you

You took me for granted
Assumed I'll always be there
While you jumped from one man to another
And you always found solace in my arms in those
intervals

I always took care of you
I always stood by you
I always loved you

But not anymore

I'm done being treated like I'm not enough
I'm done being the backup guy
I'm done being treated like I'm not worth loving

The next time you go running off
Chasing after another man
When you come back home
I'll be long gone

Every morning
I have a choice
To watch the sun rise
As it sets the sky on fire
Or I can watch you sleep
With your luscious hair ruffled
As the sun creates a halo around you
Making me believe you're an angel
An angel created just for me
To set my heart on fire
And every morning
I choose you
And I'll keep choosing you
Till the sun don't even bother to rise anymore
And my world will still be bright
Cause you're all I ever need

Do not tell me sorry in words
I can make up a song from all the sorry you've told me
Instead show me you're sorry
Paint me a picture with your actions

Show me the remorse
Show me the emotions
Show me the care
Show me the love

Don't just tell me sorry
And keep doing the same offensive acts
In a continuous cycle
Over and over again

Sorry is not a refresh button which makes it all new
Sorry is but a balm over the cut of your actions
It doesn't erase the memories
Neither does it relieve the pain

So keep your empty words
And show me you care
Before you cut through the bond between us
And no balm will soothe what isn't there anymore

Why would I give you my heart?
When you're all I've got in it
Do I give you to yourself?
Or do I keep you for myself?
This heart is mine!

Minutes becomes hours
Hours turn into days
The days merge into each other
Until weeks go by

Without you in my life
A huge chunk is missing
The integral component
The cog in my wheel

Minute pulses of color
Fading in and out
Matching the rhythm
Of my heart beat

The days go blurry
Nothing else matters
The world fades away
Leaving me alone in the dark

My soul is in chains
From a life of slavery
A world filled with pains
A heart filled with misery

Sometimes I feel like it will never end
I keep on hoping and praying
When will these sorrows ever end?
Staring at the starry night sky crying

What can I do?
To relieve these pains
What can an umbrella do?
Against these psychological rains

Your love is my sole shelter
Filling me with strength
Enough to endure every disaster
Keeping me safe through the dark night

Everyday
My heart breaks just a little bit more
I lose a tiny bit more of myself
I lose a little more of hope

Everyday
My heart becomes a little emptier
The darkness encroaches a little closer
And despair takes stranglehold of me

Everyday
I wonder what would be left of me
By the time I finally find you

I've loved and I've lusted
I've faked these emotions
But nothing I've ever done
Could have prepared me
For what I feel for you
It excites me yet scares me
It's all confusing
And makes me want to tuck my tail in
Between my legs and run
But can I ever run far enough?
It's like having peace within a war
I never know what to do
And still, I want to do it all for you
The only thing I'm ever sure of
Is that you're the sun
Around which my world orbits

You tell me I'm not worth the risk
That you're too broken
That you couldn't love me
That you can't bear the pain
If we don't work out too

You told me all these
Yet, I still stayed
Giving you my all
Hoping you learn to trust me
Hoping you learn that you'll be safe with me

At the end
You ended up breaking me too
When you decided to go with another
That you would rather risk love with another
Not caring that you broke me too

And I hope he breaks you
I hope he breaks your heart
I hope he tears your walls down
I hope he grounds your wings
I hope you feel every pain you caused me

Since I met you
You made me want to believe
In fairytales
And happily ever after

Since I touched you
You created a spark in me
From the dying embers
Of my broken heart and soul

Since I've known you
You made me feel special
Within myself
Notwithstanding my faults and lacks

Since I've kissed you
You've repaired my soul
From its fragments
Piecing together to make me whole

I've always lived my life in silence
Silence was all I knew
It was my home
Then you came along
Serenaded me with your music
Filling my ears with the most pleasurable melodies
More than I could ever imagine
When you were gone
The music went silent
The silence was back
But it was no longer my home
The silence is slowly suffocating me

Why do I care about you?
Is it your soft spoken words?
Your shy coy smiles?
Or the way I feel at home in your silence?
And the only sound is your heart beat

I wonder why I care for you so much
Trying to figure this puzzle out
But do I really want to know?
Maybe I'm just scared
Of where this road leads to

Trying to figure out this maze
Before I get lost in deeper
And be lost eternally in you
Or maybe I'll be safe
Behind these walls

The ones you've built around your heart
And I can make my home there
A home for you and I
Away from the world
Safe within your arms

All things come to an end

The good
The bad
The ugly
The beautiful

The pains you thought would be the end of you
The love you wished would last forever
They are all but passing phases

Running around in circles
With no end

Nothing comes to an end
They only change

Your love for me is so pure and true
You've got me wishing
I could go back in time
To when my love was child-like
When everything was simple
When I still believed in love
Before I felt all these pains
Before I built up these rocky walls

I know what love was
Love was the way your eyes twinkled
When you smiled at me
It was the way our hands fitted together
Like pieces of the same puzzle

The way you understood my meanings
Even when my words were all jumbled up
Love was waking up next to you
And feeling fulfilled for the rest of the day
Just cause I held you in my arms

I know what love was
Love was when I still had you
Love was what I lost
Love is a memory of you

Waking up this morning
I want to tell you
Even if you're thinking
I'm just teasing you

It doesn't make my feelings
Any less true
I've got a lot of failings
But loving you isn't one

Of all I've ever experienced
It's the greatest thing
Including all I've ever dreamed
I couldn't have ever imagined your love's sting

And how it changed my world
Bringing order and perfection
Into the chaos that was my world
With your love and affection

I want to promise you forever
An eternity of love and care
Be there for you whenever
We'll have the greatest love affair

Love and war
Love and death
They seem unrelated

But every relationship
Feels like a war

And I die a little bit
Every time my heart breaks

There's something about late night talks
That makes me feel open
That makes me feel like I can say anything

I can share;
   my greatest desires
   my grandest dreams
   my darkest secrets

I can share;
   my body
   my heart
   my soul

With you;
   there's no fear
   there's no secret
   there's only love

I always needed you
I always loved you

You never wanted me
You never loved me

I got broken
You stayed whole

Love is the sky, the sun, the moon, the stars,
the rain, the clouds on a sunny day

Love is the garden, the grass, the flowers,
the weeds, the sweet smell of autumn

Love is the storm, the wind, the thunder,
the lightening, the peace and quiet of being alone with
you

I can compare love to anything
I can compare love to nothing
The nothingness within each of us
Love is all-encompassing

Love is life
Love is death
Love is you and I
And that's all I ever needed to know

It's a delicate art
Still loving everyone I ever loved
Liked balancing a stack of dishes
One upon the other
Never learnt to unlove the ones I already loved
So they lie there simmering under the surface of the
dish water
And even when I think I'm filled up
I still find a place to love another
And when the new love breaks
It's all that comes crashing down on me
From the first to the last love
The broken slivers slashing my heart to pieces

Heart beats
Silently
Foot steps
Softly

You appeared
Mysteriously
From a dream
I never knew I had

What do I do?
To make it right
The lies and the games
That I've played on you

How do I take away the pain?
I created within you
The tears you've shed
Cause I was never there for you

Is sorry ever enough?
To make everything okay again
To ease the pain and sorrow
I caused to your heart

I'm down on my knees
Begging for your forgiveness
Hoping for another chance
To show you how much I've changed

Let me make atonement
For the previous hurts I've caused you
But I really do wonder
Will you ever love me the same?

Her smile
Is the dawning of the day
The rising of the sun
The blossoming of the flowers
The chirping of the birds

A promise of a sunny day
The slow unfolding of beauty
The delicious taste of nectar
And the mesmerizing melody of nature

You melted the ice
Embedded in my heart
With your fiery words
And passionate embraces

You transformed the frown
Fixed on my stony face
With the little things you do
Like the way you smile at me

But now

I've got rivulets of tears
Running tracks down
My weathered face
From your broken promises

My eternal love
Meant for forever
In lover's grove

My eternal love
Together we'll grow
Entwined forever

My eternal love
We'll nourish each other
Beneath the sun's glow

Loving you is a dream
Even with you next to me
It still feels unreal
And I never want to wake from it

Loving you is a dance
That I don't know the steps to
I stumble along to the beats
And hope not to trip over my own feet

Loving you is sky diving
Without parachutes or safety net
It overloads my senses with euphoria
Blinding me to my onrushing fatal end

Loving you is the silence
Between the echoes
Of your voice
As you depart into the void

Even through the pain
I'll choose you
In the pouring rain
I'll be with only you

I don't believe in an afterlife
Because you are the only life I want
Don't care about the strife
With you, I'll be alright

My love for you is eternal
Though I may bury it deep
And keep it all internal
But your thoughts invade my sleep

I don't want you perfect,
Even though I complain
With you, I have no regrets,
And you'll always be worth the pain

As I lie on my bed alone
In this cold zone
With space left for one

My thoughts wander
Into space and into the ether
And I can't help but wonder

Where are you?
Do you ache for me too?
Or are you in a bed for two?

An happily ever after
Is not in my control
But I can promise you
We'll have all the afters

The sad after
The happy after
The painful after
The pain free after

No matter the kind of after
We'll be together through them all

You kept chasing after him
Consoling him when he's heart broken
Sharing in his joys
When he thought he's found the one

A cyclic run of events
Of him finding love
Of him being heart broken

Wearing you down
Till you break down
And cry on my shoulders
Wondering why doesn't he see you

And I hold you gently
As I wonder
Why can't you see me too?

Let me leave my handprint
on your heart with neon paint
and whenever it's dark
it'll glow and light your way
back into my arms

We got our hearts merged together
With no beginning nor end
But we had a beginning
And now we've ended

But our hearts wouldn't separate easily
I had to sacrifice a part of mine
Just to make sure that yours stayed whole

You crowned me with thorns
Cause he picked all your petals
I'll bear the pain and the hurt
Till you bloom once again

I've got nothing left to say
I've got nothing left to do

I've done it all
I've said it all
Over and over again

I've given up now

TITLES

ABOUT THE AUTHOR

Pyrokardia is the pen name of Ogunfowodu Olufemi. a lover of fantasy novels, a Nigerian and a proud citizen of too many fantasy worlds. Check instagram @pyrokardia and Facebook page "PYROKARDIA" for more poems.

Made in the USA
Middletown, DE
03 May 2017